KU-223-663

Contents

How well do you handle negotiations?   iv

1 Developing negotiating skills   1

2 Using non-verbal communication   16

3 Planning your negotiation   33

4 Coping in difficult negotiations   45

5 Negotiating by e-mail   56

6 Negotiating with people from other
cultures   66

7 Negotiating the pay rise you deserve   77

Where to find more help   87

Index   89

How well do you handle negotiations?

Answer the questions and work out your score. Then read the guidance points on p. vi to find out how you can improve your negotiation skills.

How good a listener are you?
a) Poor   b) Average   c) Very good

Which word do you most associate with 'negotiation'?
a) Concession   b) Co-operation   c) Success

Do you find negotiations exciting?
a) Only if they are short.
b) If I have prepared for them.
c) Yes—as long as I get what I want.

How would you describe your approach to negotiation?
a) Defeatist   b) Prepared   c) Competitive

Is there always a winner and a loser?
a) Yes—I'm usually the loser.
b) Not necessarily—both parties can win if they're willing to compromise.
c) Yes—I'm usually the winner. I rarely give in.

How much time do you spend preparing?
a) It's usually last-minute preparation as I'm too busy.
b) As much as possible. I prioritise my objectives and try to anticipate different reactions and outcomes.
c) I know what is needed to win—that's enough.

To what extent do you use active listening skills?
a) Not much
b) As much as possible
c) Active *what*?

How would you describe your body language while negotiating?
a) Submissive   b) Communicative   c) Aggressive

What do you consider your role to be in negotiations?
a) Supporter   b) Information provider   c) Front line

How do you react when negotiations get heated?
a) I tend to panic and give in easily.
b) I usually suggest taking a break in order to let people calm down and gain some perspective.
c) I battle on and try to break down the opposition.

How do you approach your boss when it's time for a pay rise?
a) I wait for them to mention it. They know their budgets.
b) I explain how I've progressed, and why I deserve a rise.
c) I demand a pay rise—or else!

a = **1**, **b** = **2**, and **c** = **3**. Now add up your scores.

No matter how good you think you are at negotiation, you can always improve—read chapter **1** to find out how.

- **11–17:** While aggression is normally best avoided, a little more may be good for you. Instead of looking for the fastest route to a conclusion, try a little bartering and see where it takes you. Pay attention to the non-verbal signals conveyed by yourself and others—learn about these in chapter **2**. Chapter **3** offers advice for better planning, which will give you more confidence in your side of the negotiation. If you struggle with pay rise negotiations, chapter **7** should help.
- **18–26:** Although thorough preparation is your forte, be alert to the dangers of becoming complacent when you have finished preparing—an unexpected response may well be the downfall of an otherwise successful negotiation. Chapter **4** advises you on how to act in difficult negotiations, and expand your skills by reading chapter **5**, which deals with negotiating over e-mail.
- **27–33:** As a competitive person, you should try bringing a more balanced attitude to the negotiating table, and the other party will feel goodwill towards you for your ability to compromise. Remember to listen, and watch for physical signs of the other party's mood—read chapter **2** to find out how. Chapter **6** will help if you have difficulties in negotiations with other cultures.

Developing negotiating skills

We all negotiate a lot more than we think we do, in every area of our life, and developing negotiation skills is an essential part of moving up the career ladder.

Negotiation is the process of trying to find an agreement between two or more parties with differing views on, and expectations of, a certain issue. Some people dread negotiating because they associate it with conflict, bad feelings, and having to make sacrifices. However, good negotiations find a balance between each party's objectives to create a win-win outcome.

Step one: Understand the different types of negotiation

The negotiation process works by means of discussions, compromise, and 'trading'. It goes without saying that negotiations can take different forms, depending greatly on the people involved—their skills, attitudes, and style. Other factors influencing the character of a negotiation are the context or background to the negotiation, time pressures, and the issue under discussion. Negotiations tend to be competitive or co-operative, though.

1 Competitive negotiations

Competitive negotiations often have an unfriendly atmosphere and each party is clearly out to get the very best deal for themselves—the other party's objectives tend not to come into the equation. It's best to avoid this type of negotiation if possible, but if you find yourself in this situation, bear the following in mind.

✔ If you can, avoid making the opening bid as it gives a great deal of information to the other party. Try not to tell the other party too much and aim to keep control of the meeting's agenda.

✔ Conceding in a competitive situation is seen as a sign of weakness, so do this as little as possible. The size of the first concession gives the opposing party an idea of the next best alternative, and tells them exactly how far they push you.

✔ If conflict flares up, negotiators need to use assertiveness skills to maintain a prime position, and to defuse the situation.

2 Co-operative negotiations

Many people see negotiation as a battle where the stronger party defeats the weaker party, where there is a winner and a loser. In some cases, negotiations can break down altogether, such as in industrial disputes which result in strike action. In this scenario, there are only losers.

It needn't be like this, however. In co-operative negotiation, conflict is minimised and the whole idea is to reach a solution where everyone benefits. This approach tends to produce the best results, mainly because there is much better communication between the parties. In addition, it makes for better long-term relations if it is necessary to work together over a long period.

The opening will involve gathering as much information as possible but also disclosing information so solutions can be developed that are acceptable to both parties. This involves:

- considering a number of alternatives for each issue
- using open questions (which do not have 'yes'/'no' answers)
- being flexible
- helping the other party to expand their ideas about possible solutions

Both parties will make concessions if necessary, normally aiming to trade things which are cheap for them to give but valuable to the opposing party, in return for things which are valuable to them (but may not be so cheap for the other party).

TOP TIP
By listening, summarising, paraphrasing,
and disclosing in co-operative negotiations
(for example, 'I would like to ask you a

---

question. . . .' or 'I feel that I need to tell you
that. . . .'), conflict will be kept to a minimum
and it's much more likely that a solution
favourable to everyone will be reached.

Step two: Prepare yourself

As with many business situations, good preparation will help
to reduce your stress levels. Don't think that preparation
time is wasted time; it's anything but. Begin by working
out your objectives, and making sure they are specific,
achievable, and measurable. It's also important to have a
clear idea of what you are expecting from the other party.

✔ Be sure that your expectations are realistic and that
their results are easy to assess. It's a good idea to write
down objectives, ordered by priority. One way to do this
is to classify them as 'must achieve', 'intend to achieve',
and 'like to achieve'. For example, a new photocopier
has been bought for the office. It breaks down after a
week and you need to contact the supplier to sort out
the problem. The objectives can be defined as:

■ **Must achieve:** The use of a photocopier that
works.
■ **Intend to achieve:** Get the photocopier repaired.
■ **Like to achieve:** Get a replacement photocopier.

✔ Ahead of any negotiation, gather as much information
as possible about the subject under discussion. The

person with the most information usually does better in negotiations.

For example, two people have each prepared a very important document. Let's see how this situation can progress.

They both need to have them processed by the one desktop publishing operator in the firm and couriered to the destination for the following morning. However, there is only time to have one job finished before the daily courier collection at 4pm, so the two argue over whose document is the most vital. If they argue too long, neither job will be finished on time and both will 'lose'. The senior member of staff could pull rank, resulting in the junior being the 'loser', with the possible loss of his future co-operation.

If they obtained more information, they would find out that the courier company runs an optional 0pm collection which also guarantees delivery before 11am the next day. A win-win situation could then be achieved.

See chapter 3 for more information on how to prepare well.

Step three: Discuss and explore options

✔ At the beginning of a meeting, each party needs to explore the other's needs and make tentative opening offers. Remember that these need to be realistic or it's unlikely that the discussion will progress to a successful conclusion for everyone. If both parties co-operate, you can make progress; however, if one side adopts a competitive approach and the other does not, problems may arise. You need, then, to analyse the other party's reaction to what is said.

An opening statement is a good way of covering the main issues at stake for each party, and allows the discussion to develop naturally. At this stage, the issues are just being discussed and not yet negotiated. What you are trying to do is develop a relationship with the other person, so ask him or her questions to help you identify their needs and help to keep things moving.

TOP TIP
Ask 'open-ended' questions that the person can reply to fully rather than 'closed' questions to which he or she can only answer 'yes' or 'no'. For example, you could begin by saying 'Tell me your thoughts about [the issue under discussion]'.

Step four: Make a proposal

Once both parties have had a chance to assess the other's position, proposals and suggestions can be made and received. Remember that you need to trade things and not just concede them. The following phrase is valuable:

'If you (give to, or do something for, us), then we'll (give to, or do something for, you).'

✔ Look for an opportunity to trade things that are cheap for you to give but of value to the other party, in return for things which are valuable to your business.

For example, if you are a painter and decorator who needs to rent a reasonably priced flat, you could negotiate with the landlord to paint certain rooms in return for a lower rent. Or say you need to publicise a product and would like to engage someone to do some work for you, but can't quite afford to pay the job rate they had in mind. If you or your business have a website, you could offer to put a click-through link from your website to theirs so that anyone who reads their article can find out more about them and perhaps offer them more work.

Step five: Start the bargaining

After discussing each other's requirements and exchanging information, the bargaining can start (as in the example above). Generally speaking, the more you ask for, the more you get, while you'll concede less if you don't offer as much at the beginning. For example, let's say you've something to sell to another party. You know you have a premium product, but you're not sure quite how blank the other party's cheque is. If you know you'd be happy to sell for £200, you might want to start off by asking for £300, knowing that:

- you'll be able to look as if you're giving ground to the other party
- they think they're getting a bargain
- you may even get a better deal than you'd thought

If conflict arises when the bargaining starts, explain that the opening position is just that, an opening position and therefore not necessarily the one that will be adopted at the end of the negotiation.

Ultimately, an agreement can only be reached when both parties find an acceptable point somewhere between their individual starting positions.

✔ When you make an offer, be very clear about what is on the table. Avoid using words such as 'approximately' or 'about', as an experienced negotiator will spot an opportunity to raise the stakes quite dramatically. Don't make the whole process harder for yourself. For example, if you can only offer £600 for something, say so, or before you know it you'll be being pressed into agreeing to go up to £700.

✔ Similarly, when the other party makes their offer, make sure you find out exactly what it comprises. For example, if you're negotiating with a supplier, check whether the cost they are quoting you includes delivery, VAT, and so on or not. Ask for clarification if there's anything you're not sure about and check that the offer matches all the criteria that you noted down during the preparation stages as being on your list of requirements.

Step six: Communicate clearly and openly

✔ When you're negotiating with someone face-to-face, use open body language and maintain eye contact. Try to avoid sitting with your arms folded and your legs crossed, for example. This will convey an honest and friendly attitude which will help to put the other party at ease and dispel signs of defensiveness. Smiling and nodding will show the person with whom you're negotiating that you're willing to listen to their needs.

✔ Try not to use language that will annoy the other person. For example, don't use words like 'quibbling' and 'petty'. Even if you think someone is doing or being either of these things, using these words to them will only make the situation worse. Don't be sarcastic or demean them, their position, or their offer. Think through what you are about to say before you say it.

TOP TIP
If you feel that the main discussion is losing its focus and that people are starting to make asides to colleagues, be assertive and address this by saying 'I sense there's something you're unhappy about. Would you like to discuss it now?'

Step seven: Listen!

Sometimes when you are nervous about something, you become so focused on what you want to say that you don't pay enough attention to what is being said to you. This can cause all manner of problems, including knee-jerk reactions to problems that aren't really there but which you think you've heard. Active listening is a technique which will improve your general communication skills and will be particularly useful if you are often involved in negotiations. Active listening involves:

- concentrating on what is being said, rather than using the time to think of a retort of your own.
- acknowledging what is being said by your body language. This can include keeping good eye contact and nodding.
- emphasising that you are listening by summarising your understanding of what has been said and checking that this is what the communicator intended to convey.
- empathising with the communicator's situation. Empathy is about being able to put yourself in the other person's shoes and imagine what things are like from their perspective.
- offering interpretations and perceptions to help move the communication forward, then listening for agreement or disagreement. This enables both parties to start exploring the territory more openly. It is important to listen *for* at this point, which enables you to remain open

to new ideas and to think positively about the other's input. Listening *against* results in you closing down to new information and automatically seeking arguments why something won't work.

■ questioning and probing brings forth more information and will clear up any misunderstandings about what is being said.

■ not being afraid of silence. We often feel compelled to fill silences, even when we don't really have anything to say—yet silence can be helpful in creating the space to gather thoughts and prepare for our next intervention.

Step eight: Call a break if you need to

Sometimes a short break of 10 or 15 minutes may be a good thing if a negotiation is proving to be more complex or contentious than you'd expected. A break will give everyone a chance to cool down or recharge his or her batteries as necessary. It will also give everyone an opportunity to take a step back from the issue under discussion and return to the table with some ideas if there had previously been an impasse.

Step nine: Reach agreement

As the discussion continues, listen for verbal indications from the other party such as 'maybe' or 'perhaps'—these could be a sign of an agreement being in sight. Also look out for non-verbal signs, like papers being tidied away. Now is the time to summarise what has been discussed and agreed and not to start bargaining again.

Summaries are an essential part of the negotiation process. They offer a way of making sure that everyone is clear on the decisions reached and also give all participants a final chance to raise any questions they may have. As soon as possible after the negotiation, send a letter that sets out the final, agreed decision. A handshake on a deal is fine, but no substitute for a written record. Make sure your letter mentions:

■ the terms of the agreement
■ the names of those involved
■ relevant specifications or quantities
■ any prices mentioned plus discounts and so on
■ individual responsibilities
■ time schedules and any deadlines agreed

Common mistakes

✗ **You open negotiations with an unreasonable offer**
Both parties need to see a reasonable chance of getting what they want from the negotiation process. By starting off with an unreasonable offer, you risk killing the process before it starts, or at least increasing the level of mistrust.

✗ You begin negotiations without enough information about what the other party wants

The early discussion and information gathering phases need to be used properly to ensure that both parties are not 'talking past each other'. Before negotiation begins, you need to have a broad view of the points you might need to concede on, and what you want the other party to concede to you. These can then be 'traded' in accordance with your bottom line.

✗ You lose your temper

Some people are much easier to negotiate with than others and there's a difference between a serious, probing discussion and a bad-tempered slanging match laced with sarcasm. If someone is rude to you while you are negotiating with him or her, don't rise to the bait (even though it can be tempting). Instead, address them politely but assertively, and challenge their behaviour. You could say something like 'I think that comment was inappropriate and unhelpful. Shall we return to the issue?' Keep your objectives in mind at all times.

✗ You try to rush negotiations to get a quick win

Both parties need to feel comfortable with the pace and direction of negotiations as they develop. This could mean that one or other party might need time to consider certain points or options before moving on to others. You need to respect this need, while at the same time making sure that both parties observe a flexible timeframe for resolution. Endless negotiations will only waste time and money.

STEPS TO SUCCESS

✓ Understand what negotiation is about.

✓ Know the difference between competitive and co-operative negotiation.

✓ Be realistic.

✓ Prepare well before negotiations and know your objectives.

✓ Discuss your and the other party's needs when you meet and make sensible opening offers.

✓ Communicate clearly and precisely, especially when discussing figures.

✓ Listen! Negotiations aren't supposed to be a series of monologues.

✓ Call a break if proceedings get heated or you reach what seems like an impasse.

✓ When you reach an agreement, summarise and follow up in writing.

Useful links

Advisory, Conciliation and Arbitration Service (Acas):

www.acas.org.uk

iVillage.co.uk:

www.ivillage.co.uk/workcareer

Learn Direct:

www.learndirect.co.uk

Learning and Skills Councils:

www.lsc.gov.uk

Using non-verbal communication

Successful negotiation depends on good communication between the parties involved, and building rapport is vital to the effectiveness of that communication. Since non-verbal behaviour, or body language, is such a natural part of our communication toolkit, its interpretation and use offer a key to greater human understanding and relationship building.

It's widely understood that the majority of information is conveyed through non-verbal signals, most of which come from the eyes. This explains why it's often hard to convey subtle meanings over the telephone or through the written word. Because the person receiving your message can't see your body or face, your meaning may well be misinterpreted. Non-verbal communication involves many different 'channels' that convey meaning beyond what is being said. These include gestures, body movement, facial expressions, and even vocal tone and pitch. It's not an exact science, although we sometimes make judgments as if it were. Misinterpretation, especially when dealing across cultures, can have damaging consequences.

If you can learn to employ non-verbal channels consciously, you'll add a new dimension to your persuasive skills, enabling you to build rapport and influence successful outcomes in negotiations.

Researchers into non-verbal behaviour agree that between 55 and 65% of all communication is done non-verbally. It's also generally accepted that the verbal part of the communication is used to convey information, while the non-verbal part is used to convey values, feelings, and attitudes—the things that build rapport. The value of developing more than an instinctive understanding of this type of communication as well as the ability to control and use it is, therefore, clear.

Understanding body language I:
Gestures

The six most universal human emotions—happiness, anger, sadness, envy, fear, and love—can be seen on the face of anyone in the world. People smile when they're happy, scowl when they're angry, and allow their faces to drop when they're sad. Common (but not universal) gestures include a shrug for 'I don't know'; a nod for 'yes', and a side-to-side head shake for 'no'.

Gestures that you may think are universal but actually convey different messages in different cultures include the forefinger/thumb ring and the 'V' sign. Although well-established in British culture as signs for OK and victory respectively, they have offensive alternative meanings in other cultures!

Many gestures come in 'clusters'. If you look at people during a meeting, you're likely to see gestures involving hands (they may be signalling that they're evaluating what is being said by balancing their chin on their thumb with their middle finger running along their bottom lip and their index finger pointing up their cheek), their limbs (one arm may be clamped against the body by the other elbow), and their entire bodies (if someone's torso is leaning back from the vertical, that person is signalling distance from what is being said). This cluster of non-verbal gestures indicates that the listener is reserving judgment on what is being said. If you feel that a cluster of gestures is conveying something about what the person really thinks, ask them to share their thoughts.

TOP TIP

Handshakes tend to contribute to first impressions, so it's a good idea to be conscious of the different kinds. The two-handed handshake is designed to convey trustworthiness, but can send the opposite message if sincerity is lacking. The 'wet fish' or limp handshake is thought to convey weakness and lack of confidence, while the 'bone crusher'

**conveys aggression. The fingertip handshake
is interpreted as timorous and insipid. A firm
handshake, palm to palm, then a decisive
release is probably the safest bet.**

Step one: Match and mirror

If you watch two people talking in a relaxed and
unselfconscious manner, you may notice that their bodies
have taken on a similar demeanour. Both may have crossed
their legs, or settled into their chairs in similar postures. If
they're eating or drinking, they may do so at the same rate.
This is called *matching* or *mirroring*, and it occurs naturally
between two people who feel that they're on the same
wavelength.

✔ Matching and mirroring can be used consciously as a
technique to achieve rapport with someone, but you
need to be subtle. Exaggerated mirroring looks like
mimicry, and the other person is likely to feel
embarrassed or angry.

✔ Observe what your counterparts do with their bodies.
Then follow the pattern of their non-verbal
communication and reflect it back. Once this feels
natural, see if you can take the lead by changing
your body position and watch to see if they follow.
Very often they do. Once you begin to get a feel for
this process, see if you can use it in difficult situations,
such as a problematic negotiation.

Perhaps you don't have a good rapport with the person you're negotiating with, and this is causing discussions to break down. See if you can lead that person into a relaxed exchange by practising the matching and mirroring technique.

TOP TIP

Sometimes, you might inadvertently convey the wrong message—perhaps you have a habit of using an expression or gesture that is commonly accepted to mean one thing when you really mean something different. A nervous laugh, for example, might indicate that you think you're being funny. You may, in fact, be trying to communicate something serious, but are nervous because the subject is a bit delicate. Training can help correct the most obvious quirks in your non-verbal lexicon. In the meantime it might help to acknowledge your idiosyncrasies publicly so people don't get the wrong impression.

Understanding body language 2:
Facial expressions

Most non-verbal signals conveyed by the face are done so by the eyes. Good eye contact is an effective way of building rapport. Not only can you 'read' the other's disposition, you can also convey, very subtly, messages that will reinforce what you're saying.

However, too much eye contact can be intrusive or too intimate. Those who don't want to be exposed on the 'soul level' may use techniques to break or block eye contact. This includes eye movements such as the 'over the shoulder stare', or the long, fluttery, blink that effectively draws the shutters down. In a business setting, it's important to confine your gaze to the eyes and forehead, and forego the more intimate glance to the lips or upper body. If you hold your stare for too long, it may be considered hostile, so try to limit the time to around two thirds of the conversation. If you reduce the timing to below one third, you may appear timid or 'shifty'.

Eyebrows can emphasise a signal dramatically. Pulled together at the middle they can indicate a question, doubt, or concern. Both eyebrows raised up into the hairline can indicate surprise or amazement, and one eyebrow raised can indicate cynicism or suspicion.

Step two: Speak the same language

While the language we use isn't strictly one of the components of non-verbal behaviour, it's an important part of that same unconscious and instinctive toolkit we use to communicate with others. According to neurolinguistic programming (NLP)—the science of tapping into the unconscious mind to reveal what is going on beneath the surface—language can indicate a great deal about how an individual views the world. Depending on which of the five senses they subconsciously favour, people may fall into one of five noticeable types:

- visual (sight)
- auditory (hearing)
- kinaesthetic (touch)
- olfactory (smell)
- gustatory (taste)

You can establish rapport with people more effectively by paying attention to their individual preferences for 'sensual' cues.

✔ When talking to someone you don't know well, listen to the kinds of words he or she selects. Once you've identified which of the five categories (explained above) they belong to, you can respond by using the same kind of language.

In other words, when you're building rapport with someone, using the same kind of language significantly enhances the level of understanding between you.

Different types of vocabulary

Here are some examples of the vocabulary the five different types of people use:

- **visual language** includes terms like *see*, *appear*, *show*, *clear*, *picture*, *focused*, *well-defined*, *in light of*, *dim view*, *get a perspective on*, and *looks like*. For example, a person might say something like, 'I have a *vision* of what this organisation will *look* like in five years' time. I can *see* that it will take lots of energy to create what is in my *mind's eye*'. You can respond similarly: 'You build a very *clear picture* for me. I can *see* that this will be a challenge, but your *farsightedness* will surely enable you to reach your *dream*'.

- **auditory language** includes terms like *hear*, *listen*, *tune in/out*, *rumour*, *sound*, *clear as a bell*, *unheard of*, *word for word*, and *be all ears*. An auditory person might say, 'I *hear* that you've been promoted. You must have done a *resoundingly* good job!' You could respond, 'Yes, I have been *called* upon to *sound* out the market and *ring* some changes in the way we sell our products'.

- **kinaesthetic language** includes terms like *sense*, *feel*, *move towards*, *grasp*, *get hold of*, *solid*, *make contact*, *touch*, *concrete*, *pull some strings*, and *sensitive*.

- **olfactory language** includes terms like *smell*, *odour*, *rotten*, *aromatic*, and *fragrance*.

- **gustatory language** includes terms like *bitter*, *sweet*, *sour*, *salty*, and other taste-related words.

Step three: Listen actively

Active listening is a rare skill, but it's very effective in helping you communicate with other people. It can also yield valuable information, enabling us to do our jobs more efficiently.

✔ Demonstrate that you've understood and are interested in what is being said, particularly in a negotiation discussion. This kind of active listening requires good eye contact, lots of head nods, and responses such as 'Ah ha', 'Mmmm', and 'I understand what you mean'.

✔ Summarise what has been said to demonstrate your understanding, and ask open questions such as, 'Can you tell me more about . . . ?' and 'What do you think . . . ?'. These questions encourage further communication and enrich what is being communicated.

TOP TIP
People often try to cover up anger at work. However, their tone of voice, changes in facial expression, and aggressive gestures are likely to convey their real emotions. For example, maybe someone will start pacing up and down or banging the table while still smiling pleasantly in an attempt to hide their true but socially unacceptable feelings. Active listening and open questions can help to defuse anger before it boils over.

Understanding body language 3:
Props

Many people use props to reinforce their messages, the most common being extensions of the hand such as pens, pointers, or even a cigarette. Using a prop extends the space taken up by the body, and the person is perceived as more confident and powerful. It extends that person's 'territory' and sends a message distinctly different than standing with hands folded at the waist or perched on the hips.

Adjusting a tie, fussing with the hair, or tugging at a cuff is representative of 'preening'. People often use this kind of behaviour to endear themselves to others, although these gestures can instead be perceived as nervousness.

Clenching coffee cups or wine glasses close to the body allows them to be used as defence mechanisms. They effectively close off the more vulnerable parts of the body. The way people in a group sit can convey powerful messages about the pecking order. Taking the chair at the head of the table automatically puts someone in the controlling position. Leaning back with arms behind the head and one leg crossed horizontally across the other conveys feelings of superiority. A closed or crunched body position can mean disapproval, defensiveness, or a lack of interest.

Step four: Interpret in context

Much has been written about non-verbal communication, especially about how to read body language. This may give you insight into what is going on, but always remember to place your interpretation in context.

For example, someone sitting in a negotiation meeting with his or her arms crossed is possibly being defensive, reluctant, or disapproving. But bear in mind also that perhaps the person is shy, cold, or ill.

✔ Be cautious of jumping to conclusions about how someone is feeling without further information.

There is a high risk of misunderstandings at a non-verbal level if you move to a new environment or visit a workplace with a different work culture.

✔ Make sure you take time to observe what is going on around you and note how the different context makes you feel. If you can, ask advice from someone in the new culture who shares something of your own experience—they may be able to provide a useful communications bridge.

You have to be especially wary of jumping to conclusions about people's body language when conducting international negotiations. Chapter 6 deals with this topic in depth.

Understanding body language 4:
Congruence

In order for non-verbal behaviour to work for you, all the non-verbal channels of communication must reinforce the message you're trying to convey. Often, if you notice side-to-side head-shaking while someone is saying, 'I agree with this decision', you're seeing an example of incongruence; the person's words and body language are contradictory. People come across as inauthentic when one or more of their channels of communication are 'saying' opposite things.

TOP TIP

Non-verbal messages can help you spot when someone is lying. Usually, when people are communicating in a straightforward way, their non-verbal signals are consistent with their words: they might say, 'I'm unhappy about that', and their face and body will droop too. When people are bluffing, their gestures are usually inconsistent with their speech. Someone may say, 'The deal is almost in the bag!' — but you notice a nervous body pattern, like the shifting of feet or the tapping of fingers. Unusual avoidance of eye contact or a lot of blinking can also indicate an inconsistency, which communication experts call *leakage*.

Other gestures associated with lying include hiding the mouth with a hand, touching one's nose, or running a finger along the inside of a collar.

Understanding body language 5:
Territory

People travel through the world with a conceptual egg-shaped zone of personal space around their bodies, and feel invaded if others trespass into it. They often protect their territory by placing a desk between them and others, standing behind a chair or counter, or clasping an object like a handbag or briefcase to them as if it were a shield.

It's interesting to watch people in groups. If you see two or three men talking, you might notice them shifting their weight from one foot to the other. This is part of a ritual of creating territorial boundaries. They might also make themselves taller by rocking forward onto the balls of their feet to indicate power and confidence. When women are grouped, they're much more likely to mirror each other's non-verbal behaviour in an attempt to build lateral bridges.

It's essential, therefore, to place any 'bodywatching' observations *in context*, as most non-verbal communication is part of a broader dialogue.

Common mistakes

✗ **You're unsubtle**
People new to the techniques of non-verbal communication can become over-enthusiastic about it. Observe yourself objectively to make sure you aren't offending others by broadly mimicking their speech or behaviour. Remember that most people instinctively send and interpret non-verbal signals all the time: don't assume you're the only one who's aware of non-verbal undercurrents. Finally, stay true to yourself. Be aware of your own natural style, and don't adopt behaviour that is incompatible with it.

✗ **You over-interpret**
When people become aware of the power of body language, they can go overboard and think they have revealed a whole world of silent messages. However, false interpretations can cause damaging misunderstandings. Remember to take account of the context and don't jump to conclusions.

✗ **You try to bluff**
Thinking you can bluff by deliberately altering your body language can do more harm than good. Unless you're a practised actor, it will be hard to overcome the body's inability to lie. You'll be giving mixed messages and others will pick up on this.

✗ You ignore context

Putting too much store by someone's non-verbal signals can lead to misinterpretation and misunderstandings. It's important to understand the context in which the signals are being transmitted and think through the possible scenarios before jumping in. People's body language may be influenced by factors outside your relationship with them.

✗ You rush in with an accusation based on someone's body language

Accusing someone of something that they're not guilty of (if you've got the wrong end of the stick) can be embarrassing and damaging. Always check your interpretation before rushing in. If you feel someone is agitated, for example, you could say, 'I get the feeling you're uncomfortable with this decision. Would you like to add something to the discussion?' This will draw out the real message and force the other person to come clean.

✗ You over-emphasise non-verbal signals

Trying to control your meaning by emphasising your non-verbal signals can make you look ill at ease. It's very difficult to convey convincing messages that don't genuinely reflect what you think. Even if it's very subtle, leakage is bound to occur and make others suspicious. The best way to build rapport using non-verbal cues is to be authentic in what you say: your body language will reinforce that message naturally.

STEPS TO SUCCESS

✔ If you want to build rapport with someone, watch their body language and mirror it.

✔ Listen carefully to the language used by those you wish to influence. Which words and phrases do they use?

✔ Listen actively, letting the other person know you're interested.

✔ Think carefully before interpreting non-verbal signals—there could be many reasons for unusual behaviour.

✔ Look out for leakage and incongruence. They can help you identify when someone is hiding something or even lying to you.

✔ Remember that other people know about these techniques and will be able to spot any obvious attempts to influence their opinions. Be subtle!

Useful links

Body Language Expert:
www.bodylanguageexpert.co.uk
Culture at Work:
www.culture-at-work.com/nvcnegotiation.html

Changing Minds
www.changing-minds.org/techniques/body/body-language.htm

Planning your negotiation

Good planning is the first essential of successful negotiation: never give in to the temptation to 'play it by ear'. The purpose of negotiating is to give and take, to find the best deal for both parties, so you can't plan in fine detail and work from a script. There must be some room for movement and flexibility.

Step one: Be clear about your objectives

If you're about to embark on a negotiation of any kind, it's essential that you're very clear about where you're starting from and where you want to end up. Think about:

- what outcomes would be good for your organisation
- what might be acceptable
- what would be definitely *unacceptable*
- what the other party is likely to wish for/settle for/reject

✓ Think out in advance what is likely to happen and how you'll respond. It's important to protect yourself from surprises and be ready for the tactics the other party may employ. This will allow you keep the initiative and not be forced on to the back foot.

Step two: Gather all the information you need

In negotiations, information really *is* power. If you're going to commit to an agreement that affects you—or your whole organisation—then you really must have all the available information before you do so. Your task is to get as much information as you can from the other party, and have the relevant information from your side at your fingertips. This needs careful planning.

TOP TIP
Don't underestimate the amount of time you'll need to do your preparation. Try not to leave it to the last minute as you'll feel uncomfortable. You'll just be putting yourself at an extra disadvantage in what can be a stressful situation, so give yourself as much time as you can.

Step three: Understand the context of the negotiation

In commercial negotiations, the ideal outcome is almost always a win-win situation from which everybody goes away satisfied. A good deal is one that meets immediate needs, anticipates the problems, ties up the loose ends, and creates the possibility of beneficial, longer-term relationships. The key to getting deals of this kind lies in establishing a spirit of **co-operation** with the other party.

It sounds simple—but a negotiation isn't just a logical, rational conversation between two people. Every negotiation has a history and a context, things that form the backdrop to the discussion and will affect its outcome. A negotiation is a dynamic event, with different 'players' moving about the stage. There are two main 'players':

- **the people**. You and the other party aren't automatons, but normal people, subject to the many pressures and emotions of everyday life. The way you both feel about the situation, your health, personality, confidence, ambitions, and stresses will all affect the conduct of the negotiation.
- **the organisations**. Each of you is representing your own organisation, and you must both be able to sell the deal you reach to your own colleagues and bosses. The way that each of your companies 'feels' about itself, its values, recent successes or failures, past relationships with each other, business imperatives facing it, and many other factors will have effects on you—and therefore on the discussion. All these issues have to be dealt with if the organisations are to co-operate to make a deal work to mutual benefit.

✔ Gaining co-operation isn't straightforward, but a matter of balancing all these factors and finding sensible compromises. If you don't do this, there is a strong chance that you will create the opposite of co-operation which in this context is **competitiveness**. Agreements made under the influence of competitiveness don't stick: if you take advantage of the other side they will get their own back sooner or later.

There is always a temptation to be competitive and to get results at someone else's expense or to 'win' in some way. If you feel that your needs or those of your organisation aren't being met, it's easy to give in to this temptation. For example, if you perceive that the other person isn't listening to, or is dismissing, your views, you're likely to get annoyed, withdraw your co-operation and teach him or her a lesson by finding a way to score points, starting off a spiral of competitive behaviour.

Similarly, if the other person believes that you're not taking account of problems currently faced by their organisation, and pressing for a deal that you know he or she can't accept, you're likely to get a competitive response from them, and later perhaps from their organisation too. Agreement will then be much harder to achieve.

TOP TIP
Competitive behaviour can't always be avoided, so if it occurs, deal with it calmly and diplomatically, and try to move back into a co-operative position as soon as possible.

Step four: Plan for a smooth negotiation process

I Before the negotiation

✔ Think about the people and the organisations involved as part of your planning. What things are likely to influence the behaviour of each?

✔ Are there issues that need to be cleared up, or understandings reached to make the relationship work smoothly? What will be the best time to deal with these?

✔ What are *you* likely to get annoyed or upset about? What could be the 'sensitive' areas of the negotiation? Plan how to keep your cool when these issues arise.

✔ Seek information about the influences on the other organisation. How has the relationship between the two organisations been? What is known about their negotiators? Do you know the kind of people they are or what values they hold, for example? What issues are likely to be sensitive for them? How will you gain their co-operation?

✔ If you know you will have to deal with difficult matters that may affect the relationships between you and the other party, plan how you will provide 'face-savers' for them (and leverage for you) which will allow you both to close off the problem and continue to work together.

For example, you may have discovered that the other person has not been telling you the whole truth, or you need to remind them that their company let you down on a previous occasion and this cannot be accepted again.

✔ Remember that unresolved problems will land you in a competitive arena, where good deals are rarely found! Plan to prevent this as much as you can.

2 During the discussions

✔ Listen carefully to understand what is important to the other person. Try to give them enough to maintain their co-operation.

✔ If you can't do this, bring the issue out into the open, discuss its effect on the negotiation, and agree on the action needed to deal with it.

✔ If the other person becomes competitive, take care not to make the situation worse by arguing. Try responding to competitive statements with a question that will take the heat out of the situation. Look at the examples below and on the next page to see how this might work.

Dealing with competitiveness

Example 1

If someone says to you: **'I don't understand—you're deliberately trying to confuse me.'**

✗ **Don't say:** 'That's because you don't listen!'
(This is a competitive response that will cause mutual
recrimination.)

✔ **Do say:** 'I'm sorry, can you explain which
part is causing you difficulty?' (This is a
co-operative response and almost certain to get
a positive response.)

Example 2

If someone says to you: 'That's a very poor offer,
you're not trying.'

✗ **Don't say:** 'No it isn't, it's a very generous
offer!' (This competitive response will give rise to a
'Oh no it isn't'/'Oh yes it is' conversation.)

✔ **Do say:** 'Shall we just review the things we
have already agreed?' (This co-operative response
changes the focus to positive aspects of the
conversation.)

✔ Check that the other person feels able to sell the deal
you make to his or her own organisation. Help with this
if you can.

✔ Always close on a co-operative note.

3 After the negotiation

✔ Make sure that outstanding sensitivities or problem
issues are fully and quickly cleared up.

Step five: Understand the balance of power in the negotiation

If you're going to succeed as a negotiator it's important to understand the balance of power in the situation. Many inexperienced negotiators underestimate the power they have—and a few overestimate it. You need to understand your power and plan to use it wisely. It's also essential to check out the other person's power and plan how to deal with it.

There are many sources of power in a negotiation. If you have something the other party wants, you have power. At the simplest level, if the other person wants to sell you something and you have the money to buy it you have power. Ultimately you can always say 'no'! But even in this situation you may be able to increase your power by careful planning.

✔ Don't say 'yes' to an offer too early: plan to find out how badly the other party wants to sell by getting them to talk and by listening for more information. Is the price negotiable? Is money the key issue or are they looking for something else, such as a satisfied customer who will recommend them to prospective clients? Would the price be different if you bought more? Earlier? Later? Regularly? Plan ways to make the other person work hard for your business and see what emerges.

Other possible sources of power are:

Evidence	References, research, reports, and so on that back up your case. People tend to accept the written word.
Competitive edge	Is there anything you can offer that your competitors cannot?
Competence	Clearly being skilful and having done your 'homework' gives you confidence and power.
Commitment	Being passionate about your case is powerful and impresses the other party.
Risk-taking	Being prepared to take a reasonable risk gives an impression of power and confidence.
Time	If you aren't in a hurry to conclude and the other party has a time-pressure problem, you have power!
Effort	Being prepared to work hard before and during a negotiation; persistence is usually rewarded.
Money	The fact that your organisation has financial strength is a source of power.
Negotiating skills	Experience and training in negotiation is a source of power in itself.
Personal warmth	People do deals with people they like: good relationships bring power.

Remember to:

✔ Think about the power that you might have in the situation. What do you think the other person really wants?

✔ Plan questions and listen carefully to find this out early in the negotiation.

✔ Watch out for the other person using power tactics on *you*. Take your time; think about and reflect on what they are saying, and don't respond too quickly.

✔ Always test a 'firm price' or a 'take-it-or-leave-it' statement: it may be a bluff.

✔ If you *really* have no power, be prepared to walk away. No deal is usually better than a bad deal!

✔ Don't abuse your power—it will come back to haunt you.

Common mistakes

✗ Your objectives aren't clear

You need to know what you're aiming for in a negotiation before you can do any other planning. Clarifying your objectives will help you work out your tactics for the whole negotiation. If you will be working with other people on behalf of your party, make sure that you're all in agreement about your aims.

X You don't have enough information

It's essential that you spend time gathering and looking over all information relevant to the negotiation so that you're completely up to speed with the details. Don't just assume that you know all the facts—you could come unstuck.

X You don't know enough about the context of the negotiation

Understanding the context of the negotiation (that is, knowing not just what you want, but what you think the other party will want and what your respective push and pull factors are) will help you create a co-operative atmosphere more easily.

X You under- or over-estimate your power

It's important to know your strengths as you go into a negotiation, but try to be realistic about them. Don't underplay them so much that you think the other party is doing you a favour, but don't be over confident about them either, or you'll end up in a competitive negotiation.

STEPS TO SUCCESS

✔ Work out your objectives.

✔ Do your research about key facts and the context of the negotiation.

✔ Give yourself plenty of time to prepare.

✔ Try to understand the other party's needs and motivations and work with them as much as you can so that you establish a co-operative environment.

✔ Don't be tempted into a spiral of competitive behaviour if you feel the other party isn't responding as you'd hoped.

✔ Understand the balance of power in the negotiation and be aware of what you *and* the other party have to offer.

Useful link

The Negotiation Skills Company:
www.negotiationskills.com/articles.php

Coping in difficult negotiations

In spite of all your efforts to plan your negotiations well, you'll occasionally run into difficulties. The number of potential difficulties is legion, but the most common ones fall into two categories, difficult people and difficult situations.

Again, the range of possibilities is wide, but if we look at a few examples, some general principles will emerge in each case.

Step one: Deal with difficult people

People may be difficult for several reasons. They may have unresolved issues in their personal life that affect their attitudes and commitment to the negotiation. They may lack empathy and make insensitive or inappropriate remarks, or they may simply be unskilled in negotiating and make mistakes. Whatever the cause, try not to over-react and make the situation worse.

1 Decide whether you want to try to save the situation

You've had a long day and things aren't going well. Do you want to rescue what's left of the negotiation? If not, suggest postponing the negotiation to another day. If you do want to persevere, try this approach:

✓ Look at the diagram opposite. It shows two possible ways of behaving when working with others. When someone asks us for help, or appears to need it, the natural tendency of most people is to try to offer a solution. We generally produce one of the three kinds of behaviour in the top half of the diagram:

- we advise people what to do
- we tell them
- we offer to do something for them under certain conditions

This is called 'solution-centred behaviour' because it focuses principally on finding an answer. Sometimes this works, but it's all too easy to produce a brilliant solution to what later turns out to be the wrong problem. And when this happens, it is, of course, your fault!

✓ An alternative approach is to use 'problem-centred behaviour', which means going 'below the line' shown in the diagram, and questioning the other person about how he or she understands the problem.

You can do this either by **consulting** ('what exactly is the problem?', 'when did it occur?', 'what might have caused it?', and so on) or **reflecting** ('I can see that you're very angry about this, what's causing it?', 'what aspect of the problem is troubling you most?').

The key message here is to consult about **facts**, reflect on **feelings**.

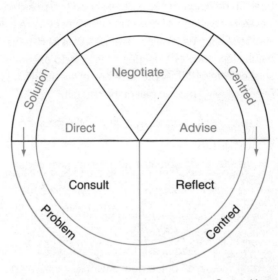

Source: Margerison

The purpose is to make sure that you both share a clear understanding of what the problem is. In fact, helping the other person to clarify his or her thinking about the problem often allows the answer to emerge as if by magic. The other party then feels as if they 'own' the solution, so they feel committed to it and you may not need to use the solution-centred behaviour at all. Even if the answer does not appear automatically, though, you can now direct or advise from a much better understanding of the issues.

2 Tap into the power of questions

The key to the 'below-the-line' approach is that it obliges
you to ask questions, which is always a good idea if you
have to deal with difficult people as it enables you to control
the conversation—if you ask a question, people will usually
answer it. This approach avoids confrontation, and it may
get you valuable information about the person or the
negotiation.

We can see the value of this approach in the following
anecdote.

In the United States, there is a club called Salesmasters,
which is a group of super salespeople who have made
negotiation an art. One of their number was being
interviewed on a TV chat show by a presenter who
was very hostile and intent on rubbishing the idea that
selling is a skill.

He said to the salesperson: 'It's all a confidence trick
played on the gullible. You couldn't sell me anything—
that, for example.' He pointed to a large ashtray on the
table between them.

The salesperson looked at him and said: 'Why would
anyone want an ashtray like that?'

Rather to his surprise, the presenter went into a long
diatribe about the fact that he did not smoke, but others
who did were constantly leaving ash all over his carpet
and sometimes put the butts in his potted plants, and so

on. If he had the ashtray, at least they would know where to put their nasty, smelly rubbish.

When he had finished, the salesperson looked at him and said: 'That's really interesting. And what would you give for an ashtray like that?'

'Oh . . . about $5', said the presenter.

The salesperson picked up the ashtray and handed it to the presenter with the words: 'I think I could let you have it for that. We have a deal!'

Two questions, and the most determined opposition disappeared!

3 Remember the guidelines

✔ When in doubt go 'below the line' and consult and reflect.

✔ Ask good, useful, open questions: plan them carefully.

✔ Ask for the other party's proposals or ideas—don't give yours first.

✔ Ask for clarification of the other party's proposals rather than saying what is wrong with them.

✔ Ask about their goals and objectives rather than telling them about yours.

✔ Ask how you can help them.

TOP TIP
Be subtle! If the other person spots
what is going on he or she might
feel manipulated—so keep your
questioning within reasonable limits.

4 Have a back-up plan if all else fails

If the other person is still being 'difficult' and hindering the
negotiation, more drastic action is needed. Either he or
she doesn't want the negotiation to succeed, or is unable
to conduct the discussion properly at this time. In any
case, you need to do something to move things along.

✔ Acknowledge that there seems to be a problem.

✔ Ask three key questions:

- Does he or she want to continue the discussions?
- Would it be better if you spoke with someone else?
  A more senior member of staff, for example?
- Is there anything you can do that will help him
  or her feel more comfortable with the negotiation?

Step two: Deal with difficult situations

Not all negotiations take place face-to-face these days
and, in fact, most negotiations happen over the phone
or by e-mail. Chapter 5 gives you detailed information

on how to negotiate by e-mail, but here we'll look at negotiating by phone. People sometimes opt for this to save time, but it's very much a second-best situation: avoid it as much as possible, except for simple negotiations.

For these straightforward discussions, telephone contact can have certain advantages:

- it's relatively cheap and usually quite quick
- you can spread your papers out in front of you for easy reference—this is especially useful if you need to refer to price-lists, discounts, and so on
- you can use check-lists to act as prompts
- you can take notes or make calculations as you wish
- the telephone forces you both to listen well
- decisions can be made promptly

However, there are a number of general disadvantages for both parties, but particularly for the party that has not initiated the discussion. You need to take account of these if put in this situation. The main problems are:

- you have little time to think
- you get no 'feel' for the other person, because you can't see them, and you can't pick up on any non-verbal clues in their behaviour
- the telephone is impersonal; it is difficult to use the 'personal domain'
- many standard negotiation tactics are less effective over the phone

- it's difficult to set and keep to an agenda
- people are more inclined to say 'no' on the phone because they don't get that little extra reassurance that comes from face-to-face contact
- 'what if. . . .?' questions and searches for a 'better deal' can be more difficult on the phone—there is a tendency to stick to the specified business.
- it can be difficult to co-ordinate within your own organisation
- there is a danger of distractions: visitors, noise, pending appointments, and so on
- many people feel pressured by time during a phone call: it's difficult to digest information slowly, reflect, and re-organise your thinking on the hoof
- silences are more threatening in a phone call (and in some countries, may lead to the connection being lost)
- you feel as if you have been pushed into making decisions too quickly
- the line may be bad, disrupting the flow of the negotiation, and you don't know who else is listening
- if you forget something, it may be difficult to come back to the point or introduce it later: telephone calls tend to be 'linear' (that is, you may only have one opportunity to say or raise something), whereas face-to-face conversations can go round in loops

If you *have to* negotiate over the phone:

✔ arrange a time that will allow you to do some preparation beforehand. If someone 'ambushes' you and you're caught off guard, ask if you can ring them back in half an hour or so.

✓ have all the necessary paperwork close at hand. For example, if you're discussing the renewal of a contract, make sure you've a copy close by that you can refer to. Also have plenty of paper nearby that you can make notes on.

✓ make sure that you won't be disturbed. If you have an office, close the door. If you work in an open-plan office, see if you can book a meeting room elsewhere in the building so that you won't distracted by other people's conversations around you.

✓ even though the other party can't see you, use the body language you would use if they were there in person, for example nod if you agree, move your hands as you speak. All of this will filter back in the tone of your voice.

✓ ask someone to sit in with you if you feel you might need some back up.

✓ take a break and arrange to call the other person back if things are getting heated or you've reached a stale-mate.

✓ once agreement has been reached, follow up in writing as you would do if you'd conducted a face-to-face negotiation.

Common mistakes

✗ You battle on when it's just not worth it

While everyone aims to tie up negotiations with the least amount of fuss and wasted time possible, some days it just won't work. On those days, it's important to recognise this, cut your losses, and rearrange for another time.

✗ You don't get to the bottom of why someone is being 'difficult'

Even though your patience may be stretched to its absolute limit, try to put yourself in the other party's shoes to find out why they are acting in the way that they are. Also ask questions that allow the other party to disclose their concerns and motivations—you may actually be able to help them, thus achieving that ideal win-win goal.

STEPS TO SUCCESS

✔ Work out if the situation is worth saving.

✔ If things have gone too far, consider postponing the negotiation to another day.

✔ If it is worth carrying on, try to work out whether solution-based or problem-based behaviour will help salvage the discussion.

✔ Ask useful, 'open' questions that allow the other party to respond fully and convey to you why they are being 'difficult'.

✔ Ask for the other party's views and ideas.

✔ Be subtle!

✔ Have a back-up plan.

Useful link

The Negotiation Skills Company:
www.negotiationskills.com/articles.php

Negotiating by e-mail

A huge number of commercial negotiations today are conducted via e-mail, a process which has both advantages and disadvantages and needs careful handling to get it right.

The speed of online communication means that we can sometimes resolve issues more quickly than we might have done when face-to-face meetings were the only way forward. E-mail also allows us to contact people all over the world with relative ease, so rather than having to pick our way through erratic phone connections and time zones, we can send a message in the reasonable hope that the right person will get it.

However, 'virtual' negotiation misses out on many of the subtleties of negotiation we take for granted in a face-to-face meeting. When we negotiate in this way, a lot can be conveyed by our tone of voice, body language, and facial expressions. So the e-mails you use in this context need to work quite hard to get the same results. This chapter sets out to equip you with the basic skills that will help you achieve great results in spite of the disadvantages of 'virtual' negotiation.

Step one: Remind yourself about the principles of negotiation

Whether you negotiate face-to-face, over the phone, or by e-mail, the overall principles do not change. In basic terms, negotiation is a process with the aim of finding a balance between the objectives of two or more parties.

Before and during a negotiation:

✔ **prepare well.** Make sure you have all the facts to hand and have read any related correspondence so you're completely up to date with the situation. Keep (and print out if you need to) all previous e-mails relevant to the negotiation in case you need to refer to them if any queries arise.

✔ **be sure of your own objectives.** Work out your ideal scenario, a realistic scenario (that is, one that is not ideal but with which you'd still be pleased), a fallback position (that is, one that is some way removed from the ideal scenario, but which still offers something of value), and an absolute minimum resolution.

✔ **be clear and request clarification from others.** Try to convey exactly what your position is and avoid words such as 'approximately' or 'about' so that there is absolutely no room for confusion. Similarly, if you feel unsure about what the other party is offering you, ask them to explain again.

✔ **be prepared to be flexible.** If you expect others to compromise, you need to be ready to compromise yourself.

✔ **summarise as appropriate** so that everyone is clear about what has been agreed and what further action is required (if any).

Step two: Compose the opening offer

✔ If you or your party are making the first move in the negotiation, begin by sending an e-mail to explore what the other party's expectations and ideal outcomes may be. Once you know those, and what your ideal response would be, write a well-structured e-mail that sets out:

- your offer
- prices/discounts where appropriate
- deadlines where appropriate
- any issues that are non-negotiable for legal reasons

✔ To make the e-mail easier to read, make each of these points a separate heading and use a bold font to make them stand out even more. Avoid italics if you can as some people find them hard to read, especially on-screen.

Step three: Manage the correspondence

In some cases, an e-mail negotiation can be a simple process, involving one party making the opening offer and the other party agreeing immediately to the suggested terms. In other cases, it may be more protracted if each party has queries on the other's position or requests.

If you find yourself in this situation, you need to manage the correspondence well to keep the negotiation on track and reach a resolution that works for everyone. For example, let's look at how a customer complaint may progress through a company:

- The first e-mail from the customer sets out his or her complaint.
- In your initial reply, you acknowledge the complaint and either offer an explanation or an apology, or advise the customer that you want to investigate further.
- If you are investigating further, give the customer an approximate date for your detailed reply.
- In your detailed reply, give a full explanation and tell the customer what you are offering by way of apology or compensation.
- If the customer does not accept the explanation or the offer, you may have to take the negotiations further.
- If necessary, you can e-mail copies of all correspondence to a colleague or someone else who may be able to resolve the situation.

TOP TIP
Throughout the process, keep copies of all
e-mails so that you can refer to earlier
correspondence if circumstances change.
However, it is not necessary to include
all the previous correspondence in
each e-mail you send—this is known as
the 'thread' and it can become unwieldy.

Step four: Keep your cool

Sometimes, tempers fray during negotiations. The
discussions may take longer than planned, unexpected
problems may have arisen, and energy levels (as well
as patience) can flag. Under these circumstances it's
important to keep calm, otherwise you run the risk of
jeopardising the whole negotiation process.

✓ Adopt a polite but firm tone in all formal communications,
particularly during negotiations, even if you have to
deal with difficult or angry customers. It's all too easy to
reply hastily to an angry message and communicate
information that you may regret later.

✓ If you're angry about something, wait before replying.
This will give you time to cool down and also to re-read
what was actually sent to you: in the heat of the moment,
you may have misread the message.

TOP TIP

If you are replying to a badly written or unclear
e-mail, maintain your own high standards
and be sure that your message is polite
and has no spelling or punctuation errors.
As a rule of thumb, make sure that any
e-mails you send as part of a negotiation
are ones that you would not be ashamed
to show to your manager.

✔ If the incoming message is unclear, don't be afraid to
ask the sender for clarification. It's better to be 100%
sure of your grasp of the situation than to embark on a
protracted correspondence that will come undone at the
last minute when a major misunderstanding comes to
light. A simple 'please could you explain . . . in more
detail' should sort out any uncertainties.

TOP TIP

As in face-to-face negotiations, some
people are easier to deal with than
others. If you receive e-mails that are
persistently rude or angry from the
same source, you need to address the
problem. Don't stoop to their level
and escalate the situation by adopting
the same tone: this is known as
'flaming' and is strongly discouraged in
e-mail etiquette. Instead, use polite but

assertive language to make clear that rudeness is unacceptable, such as 'I understand your concerns but I believe that we can resolve the matter more easily if we communicate calmly'.

Step five: Watch your tone

As described above, e-mail negotiations can founder because the correspondents miss out vital clues that they would normally pick up in face-to-face or even telephone discussions, such as what your body language or tone of voice is indicating. While you're negotiating by e-mail, think carefully about *what* you say and *how* you say it.

TOP TIP
If you're writing a particularly tricky or delicate message, it's a good idea to write a draft first, do something else for half an hour and then come back to it. You could ask a trusted colleague for a second opinion before sending it.

Although your correspondents can't hear what you're saying, they can certainly pick up an impression of your mood by what you write. In your messages, try to avoid words such as 'petty', 'trivial', 'quibbling', and 'stalling'. Even if you think the opposite party is doing some of these things, you won't be helping by emphasising this.

TOP TIP
Don't use capital letters or multiple exclamation marks to emphasise a point. Even if what you're saying isn't aggressive or inflammatory, the way your message looks (especially at a quick first glance) may confuse or antagonise your correspondent.

Step six: Summarise and conclude

An important stage in any negotiation is a summary when the negotiations are over and agreement has been reached. This gives everyone an opportunity to review the decisions and to be sure that they are happy with them.

Circulating a summary by e-mail is fine, especially for internal negotiations, but you may want to follow up by letter if you've been dealing with an external client.

TOP TIP
Try to write your summary as soon as you can after the negotiation has been concluded so that you can easily remember all the decisions. The longer you leave it, the more painful a process it will be!

Common mistakes

✗ You don't take enough care composing your messages

Time is at a premium for all of us, but it's well worth spending as much time as you can over your messages when you're negotiating by e-mail. Whether you're composing your initial offer or trying to seal the deal, check over your message before you send it to make sure that it's completely clear, polite, and has no spelling mistakes. If you have some spare time, leave your message for a few minutes and then come back to it—you're bound to spot something you've missed.

✗ You send a message you regret

If you lose your temper while you're negotiating and fire off an e-mail that makes your mood very clear to your recipient, you've some work to do. Apologise as quickly as you can (it's probably best to do this by telephone) and try to establish a co-operative atmosphere again. You can do this by recapping what you have agreed on, as this will remind the other party that you're not always unreasonable!

STEPS TO SUCCESS

✔ Spend as much time as you need in preparation before negotiating.

✔ Make sure you are aware of all relevant facts.

✔ If your party is making the opening offer, write a simple, clearly-structured e-mail setting out your position.

✔ Ask for clarification if you need it when you receive the counter-offer.

✔ If your correspondent becomes aggressive, don't reply in anger. Draft a reply and cool down before you send it.

✔ Remember that e-mail negotiation can't rely on the visual or physical 'clues' that face-to-face negotiation can, so be careful not to use language that will annoy the other party.

✔ Summarise and conclude by letter if appropriate.

Useful link

Emailreplies.com:
www.emailreplies.com

Negotiating with people from other cultures

With business becoming global and increasing numbers of international mergers and acquisitions taking place, it probably won't be long before you find yourself having to negotiate with people from other cultures. Seeking new customers or business partners overseas is the obvious example, but receiving potential clients or suppliers from overseas or even doing business with other parts of your own company—if it's multinational—will involve you in cross-cultural negotiations.

Remember that it's not up to the other person to adapt to *you*: not attempting to understand and take account of the other party's cultural background may be felt as an insult. On the other hand, most people *will* notice if you make the effort and give you generous credit for it.

The best way to prepare for cross-cultural negotiations is by living in the other culture, or by finding a reliable local mentor or partner. However, if you're not able to do this, there are things that you can do to improve the probability of success and minimise the risk of mistakes. Careful planning and attention will pay dividends.

Step one: Investigate social conventions

Wherever you're travelling to on your business trip, finding out more about the social conventions of a country or region is invaluable.

Obvious differences in cultural style are easy to spot, but it's the more subtle distinctions that usually cause problems. For example, unintended rudeness or failure to observe little politenesses can quickly make the negotiations competitive. There are a small number of general areas in which these subtleties usually occur, so observe these things carefully when you're in the country, and investigate them as much as you can beforehand.

1 Meeting and greeting procedures

Watch how these work. For example, you need to think about:

- who introduces whom
- whether gestures such as bowing are appropriate
- whether you're expected to shake hands, and if so, how
- whether women shake hands
- whether there are set greetings and responses

✔ As a general rule, hold back. It's wise to be guided by your hosts and avoid any physical contact until you're sure it's acceptable. While most people will appreciate any attempt you make to speak their native language, don't be too enthusiastic in adopting local customs—it may make some cultures suspicious and feel that you're mimicking them, rather than trying to match your approach to fit theirs.

Watch your (body) language!

Remember that a lot of the non-verbal clues we give to our colleagues or friends when we communicate with them won't always travel that well to other countries. While a smile can rarely go wrong, bear in mind that some cultures:

- find the 'ok' sign (that is, thumb and forefinger closed together to make a circle) offensive.
- also find the 'thumbs up' sign offensive.
- think that standing with your hands on your hips (as many people do in repose) means that you're angry.
- are less offended by a lack of personal space than others. For example, you may find that people may come and stand right up close to your face while they're talking to you. This can be disconcerting if you're not expecting it.
- prefer a kiss on both cheeks to a handshake.
- value silence more than others. In the West, we often feel duty-bound to fill any gaps in a conversation with chit-chat, whereas in Japan, for example, silence is important and designates 'thinking time'. In the

context of a negotiation, saying too much is a bad move. Say only what you really need to.
■ are reluctant to make eye contact as they feel it's insulting. This is particularly the case among some Latin American and African countries.
■ get to the point more quickly than others. In some countries, there may be a long exposition to the negotiation that you may find frustrating if you're in a rush. Be patient, however, and adjust to a different pace.
■ are offended by people who chew gum or keep their hands in their pockets during conversations.
■ are much more tactile than others.
■ won't sit with their legs crossed (as many people do to show they are at ease) as this may mean that the sole of their shoe is pointing at someone. This can be considered extremely rude and should be avoided.

2 Ideas about time

Observe local customs about timing of meetings, particularly:

■ the rules about appointments. Do you turn up *on* time (Europe); *before* time (China); or a little *after* time (Africa)?
■ how time is used—rigidly or flexibly? Does a half-hour appointment mean exactly 30 minutes, or anything up to an hour?
■ how your host will indicate that your time is up. How and when you can politely take your leave?

3 The role of women

Some cultures have embraced the role of women in business more than others, and may have very clear conventions governing gender relationships. You need to know:

■ how women's roles are defined in the country you're visiting. Don't comment on this, whatever your views may be.
■ the level of women's involvement in business
■ any 'rules' covering relationships between men and women at work and socially

4 Eating and drinking etiquette

In many cultures, communal eating may have its own set of symbolic social rituals. Sometimes these are based on religion, sometimes on historical tradition. If you're invited to a meal, find out beforehand from a reliable source what the etiquette is, particularly:

■ what form the meal will take, that is, whether it's formal or informal
■ customs such as washing, which hand to use when eating, formal ceremonies, if there are prayers before meals, and so on
■ what people normally drink with their food (that is, whether alcohol is permissible or not)
■ whether it's polite to eat/drink everything or whether you should leave something on your plate

- whether business is discussed over meals
- any dress conventions

TOP TIP

**Watch what others do and be guided by them.
For example, don't be offended if people lean
over and help themselves from your plate—
this is polite in some cultures!**

---

5 Gifts

This can be a sensitive area: some cultures will tend to
perceive a gift as a bribe, others as an embarrassment.
Therefore, find out:

- what is the attitude to gifts—are they accepted or
  expected?
- the type of gift that is appropriate. Be particularly careful
  about gifts to one's host or hostess if invited to
  someone's home
- customs for receiving gifts yourself

This is one of those areas where no one will notice if you get
it right, but everyone will be aware if you get something
wrong!

6 Humour

Don't make jokes until you're sure you understand the jokes
made by the other party! Be aware that irony or sarcasm

often isn't picked up easily by people who don't share your first language, so don't take refuge in either of them too much.

If the worst comes to the worst and you feel you've made a gaffe, don't try to 'rescue' the situation by making another joke. It's best to just move on and pick up the threads of your earlier conversation or start a new one.

Step two: Understand business practices

Although there's increasingly a common core to conducting business internationally, there are certain important conventions and habits that distinguish one culture's way of doing business from another. If you're working in new markets you need to make sure that you're aware of any cultural differences that might have an impact on the outcome of your negotiations.

I National characteristics

Since the end of the Cold War many new countries have been created—and new markets opened up for business. Some of these countries have no recent history of dealing with foreigners and little experience of international trade, so doing business there can be very tough. But forewarned is forearmed: find out what you can about cultural attitudes and be ready to deal with them patiently. Look particularly at:

- their understanding and acceptance of outsiders
- who controls business and how it works
- how decisions are made. Is the culture one where compromise is sought or is it more competitive?
- how their legal, technical, and financial systems differ from your own. Are there any special conditions that will have to be met?
- whether support systems (transport, banking arrangements, and so on) are adequate to deliver the deal, and does the other party have reasonable control of them?

2 Language

Negotiate in your own language if you can: fluency gives power, but be aware that the other side has already made a concession to you!

✔ Don't underestimate the dangers of missing subtle points when you have to work in another language. Use this to your advantage: slow things down, ask for clarification frequently.

✔ In most cultures you will 'gain points' for speaking their language—but many will be less forgiving of 'cultural errors' if you do. You might decide not to disclose your knowledge of their language if it isn't fluent.

✔ Confirm all concessions: check for accidental misunderstandings.

✔ If you work in your own language, check regularly that the other party has understood you properly. Use questions or summaries to do this.

3 Working with an interpreter

If you feel it's appropriate, hire an interpreter. Make sure that he or she:

- is professionally neutral and properly skilled
- understands what negotiating is about and what the objectives of this negotiation are
- can translate not just words but also meanings through gestures, tone of voice, and so on

✔ Rehearse with your interpreter to create familiarity with likely events.

✔ Don't accept the other party's interpreter if the negotiation is an important one.

✔ Plan plenty of breaks: long negotiations in a foreign setting are very tiring.

Step three: Keep the basics in mind

✔ Don't be in too much of a hurry. Give yourself plenty of time to deal with the unexpected, to recover from travel, get used to the climate, and so on.

✔ Decide under whose law contracts will be applied (preferably your own). If you have to accept the other party's law, check out the implications carefully.

✔ Be sure that technical, professional, safety, and environmental standards accord with the other party's national standards, and are acceptable to your own company.

✔ Make sure you've established a good line of communication with your home base.

✔ Don't try to take on the style of the other culture. Be aware of it, but retain your own (cultural) style and play to your strengths.

Common mistakes

✗ **You think you can wing it**
Taking the time to find out more about another culture may seem like a bind, but any preparation you do will be put to very good use. Imagine how embarrassed you'd be if a negotiation came to nothing because of a gauche remark or gesture you made. Courtesy is essential in business: you would expect it of others, and they will expect it of you.

✗ **You try to cover uncertainty with jokes**
Remember that some jokes just won't work when translated into another language, and may make things

worse if a situation is getting heated. Err on the side of caution if you're meeting someone for the first time or if the negotiation is particularly fraught.

STEPS TO SUCCESS

✔ If you're negotiating abroad or with others from a different culture, find out as much as you can about their way of doing things beforehand.

✔ Observe meeting and greeting conventions.

✔ Watch your body language as well as your verbal communication.

✔ Investigate eating and drinking etiquette in case you're invited for a meal.

✔ Be very careful if offering a gift to the other party.

✔ Negotiate in your own first language if you can. If not, hire an impartial interpreter.

Useful links

BusinessCulture.com:
www.businessculture.com
ExecutivePlanet.com:
www.executiveplanet.com

Negotiating the pay rise you deserve

One potentially difficult area of negotiation that we all have to deal with is agreeing a payrise. Many people feel awkward when discussing money, but remember that if you're not willing to sit down and negotiate, the chances are that your employer will have no qualms about paying you the bare minimum.

When you make your request, it's very important to think through the issues outlined in this chapter and have lots of information available. It's also important to know how to respond if you end up receiving a negative answer.

Step one: Choose your moment

The most obvious time to ask for a pay rise is during your performance review with your boss. However, it's not uncommon for supervisors to put off these discussions for quite a while. It's one of their least favourite things to do.

✔ If it's been more than a year since your last performance review and since your last salary increase, you should approach your supervisor about discussing your performance and salary. Don't try to by-pass this discussion by presenting your case in a letter. This may come across as cowardly or confrontational. Remember that negotiation is a two-way process.

✓ Give your boss time to prepare his or her thoughts for this discussion. Don't put them on the spot by asking for a meeting in front of other employees, and don't just drop into his or her office and say, 'I'd like to talk to you about giving me a pay rise'. If your supervisor is caught unprepared, they will feel uncomfortable. More importantly, they may not have the information they need to give you a definitive answer.

✓ Tell your supervisor that you'd like to have a meeting to discuss your performance, your career plans, and your salary, and plan for it to last at least 30 minutes.

TOP TIP
All companies go through boom times and difficult times, and they tend to retrench and cut costs when things are difficult financially. But that doesn't mean that you can't ask for a pay rise. If you've done a really outstanding job this past year and can point to concrete contributions, it's possible that the company might be able to find some money or other form of benefit to reward your hard work.

Step two: Document your achievements

When you ask for a pay rise, you need to build a business case for why the company should pay you more. You need to show what you've done for them and document why they should reward you.

It's easy to forget all that you've done, but if you keep track of your achievements along the way, you'll have an excellent record of what you've contributed.

✔ Keep a job diary or a file of your contributions to the company throughout the year. Be sure to keep track of measurable results from your actions, such as money saved, sales increased, level of quality improved, or percentage of employee retention.

✔ Prepare a one-page executive briefing on your accomplishments to take into your meeting.

If you go into the salary negotiation meeting with well-prepared documentation of your achievements, you'll have a stronger sense of your worth to the company and will feel more self-assured about asking for a pay rise.

TOP TIP
If you're still nervous, consider asking someone to role-play the situation with you so that you can practise beforehand. It's also helpful to visualise the meeting

---

ahead of time and to picture what success would look like. Eliminate any negative talk in your head such as, 'No one ever appreciates what I do,' or 'I never get what I want,' and replace these ideas with something positive such as, 'I've worked hard for this company this past year, and I can present a strong case for why I should receive a pay rise.'

Step three: Know your worth in the marketplace

Organisations make a trade-off between paying enough money to keep people motivated and the desire to minimise labour costs. You need to be your own agent and promote your own case. If you don't look out for yourself, the chances are that no one else will.

When companies calculate how much they should pay for a job, they conduct wage surveys to compare salaries within the industry and geographical area. They also conduct internal pay analyses to make sure that comparable jobs within the company receive comparable pay. Such wage and salary information is now available on the Internet (see 'Useful links' on p. 86).

Negotiation is much easier if you know the sort of figure you can reasonably aim for in the current market. Calculating your market value can also be a good confidence booster.

✔ As well as researching your market value externally, try to find out information about the internal pay structure. If you have a human resources department you can ask them for information on what jobs like yours typically pay.

✔ Approach your meeting with your supervisor with a win-win attitude. Your goal is to get a pay rise. Your supervisor's goal is to have a highly motivated and productive employee.

✔ Remember that pay rises are never given for potential or for what you're 'going to do'. Pay rises are given for meeting and exceeding performance goals. When you meet with your supervisor, you should be thinking about how your actions and accomplishments have helped to fulfil your supervisor's own goals.

TOP TIP

It's helpful to learn about the salary philosophy of your organisation. For example, does it pay the minimum it can to keep costs down, or does it pay higher than the market rate in order to attract the best employees? Does it tend to give pay rises close to the cost of living increase for the year (which isn't really a pay rise)? Does it require managers to create a hierarchy among their staff and only give pay rises to the highest performers? If you have an understanding of the company philosophy, you can come to your salary discussion well prepared.

Step four: Discuss, don't dictate

When the meeting begins, remember to build your case—
don't rush straight into a request for money. If you've
provided evidence to support your claims, it will be much
harder for your boss to turn you down.

Equally, be ready to pick up any valuable career tips your
boss may offer. This should be a two-way discussion, not
a one-way tirade.

✔ Start your negotiation with a description of your
   accomplishments and contributions, moving into a
   discussion of how you intend to build on those in the
   coming year, and what some of your key goals are.
   Describe your goals in terms of how they will support
   your boss and make a difference to the company.

✔ Ask for the amount and percentage of salary increase
   that you think you deserve and explain why.

✔ Listen to any objections your boss may have. Consider
   this discussion as a mentoring session and keep an
   open mind about what you can learn that will help your
   progress in the company.

✔ Before trying to overcome any objections, make sure
   that you communicate your understanding of those
   objections by paraphrasing what you've heard. This is
   the first step in negotiation.

✔ Be ready for objections and be prepared to explain why you still deserve a pay rise.

✔ If a salary increase looks unlikely, suggest acceptable alternatives: perhaps you'd like some extra holiday time, a change in working conditions, training, or improved benefits. However, if money is your main concern, stay focused on salary as far as possible.

TOP TIP

If you're offered a promotion instead of a pay increase, consider all the factors before you decide whether to accept. First of all, make sure it isn't just a change of job title. If the promotion increases your skills, your responsibilities, and your visibility, and if the company is a start-up or is otherwise strapped for cash, you might agree to take it. But also get written agreement from your supervisor that you'll have a salary discussion at a predetermined time in the future, such as three months.

Step five: Accept the decision

There's a possibility that your negotiations won't be successful. This could be for reasons beyond your or your boss's control, so it may not be a reflection on your own performance or abilities.

✔ If you're told that you won't be getting a pay rise at this time, ask what it is you need to do in order to earn an increase. Write down everything you're told.

✔ After the meeting, write a memo thanking your boss for their time, and listing the actions you need to take in order to earn a pay rise.

Common mistakes

✘ **You threaten to leave if they don't give you a pay rise**

Unless you're really unhappy and were thinking of leaving anyway, this strategy can do you much more harm than good. If you threaten to leave, you're sending the message that you aren't committed to the organisation and are basically out for yourself. This approach isn't likely to enhance your career.

✘ **You complain to colleagues about your salary**

Most organisations prefer that all salary discussions take place only with your immediate supervisor. If you complain about your salary to your colleagues, you're seen as someone who isn't a team player, and who isn't politically astute. It's unlikely that you'd be promoted or get a pay rise under these circumstances.

✘ **You ask fellow employees how much they make**

Unless you're in an 'open-book' company, most organisations prefer that salary information be kept private. They're concerned that if employees begin to compare salaries with one another, it may lead some to think that they're being treated unfairly and therefore lead to lower morale. You can get a better idea of your worth by benchmarking similar jobs in your organisation and then doing a search on the Internet for salary ranges for those jobs.

STEPS TO SUCCESS

✔ If you feel that you deserve a pay rise, resolve to do something about it!

✔ Don't rush into the negotiations. Give yourself and your boss time to prepare.

✔ Gather evidence to support your case.

✔ Get an idea of the kind of figure you should ask for.

✔ Stay calm in the meeting itself. Treat it as a conversation, not a battle.

✔ Have an alternative suggestion if a pay rise is out of the question.

✔ If you don't succeed, learn from the experience. Find out why you didn't get the pay rise this time and what you need to do to succeed next time.

Useful links

Businessballs.com:
www.businessballs.com/payrise.htm
Monster.co.uk:
http://content.monster.co.uk/salaries_benefits
SalarySearch:
www.salarysearch.co.uk

Where to find more help

Difficult Conversations
Douglas Stone, Bruce Patton, Sheila Heen
London: Penguin, 2000
272pp ISBN: 014027782X
This book aims to help readers to become calm and assertive in difficult situations (such as asking for a pay rise, or experiencing problems with colleagues). In discussing the different emotions and requirements that arise from such conversations, the book aims to pinpoint ways of managing them more effectively.

Doing Business Internationally 2nd ed
Danielle Walker, Thomas Walker
Maidenhead: McGraw-Hill Education, 2002
280pp ISBN: 0071378324
As well as covering the basic skills necessary for becoming culturally competent, this book offers in-depth analyses of six world regions, techniques for minimising the impact of cultural differences in business, and models for understanding the hidden forces that guide institutions, behaviour, and interactions. It also provides a 'Cultural Orientations Inventory' — a tool for identifying and correcting one's cultural skills gaps.

Getting Past No
William Ury
London: Random House Business Books, 1992
172pp ISBN: 0712655239
This book provides a step-by-step method for negotiation that aims to ensure that satisfactory agreement is reached with even the most intransigent people. It contains advice, hints, and tips, useful strategies, and plenty of real examples.

Getting to Yes
Roger Fisher, William Ury, Bruce Patton
London: Random House Business Books, 2003
224pp ISBN: 1844131467
By working around four main principles of effective negotiation and discussing the difficulties that can arise, the authors show the reader

how to pursue his or her own interests while keeping adversaries happy at the same time. A few principles will guide the reader no matter what the other side does, or whatever what tricks they may resort to.

I Win, You Win
Carl Lyons
London: A & C Black, 2007
224pp ISBN: 9780713677058
Focusing on principled negotiation, this book offers techniques to help you build strong, lasting relationships. It covers how to understand each party's motivations, build rapport, tune into body language & communicate clearly.

Secrets of Power Negotiating 2nd ed
Roger Dawson
Franklin Lakes, NJ: Career Press, 1999
320pp ISBN: 1564143996
This practical book shows readers how to win negotiations while leaving the other party feeling as though they have won too. Taking the reader through the whole process from beginning to end, the author includes advice on how to recognise unethical tactics, how to negotiate with people from different cultures, and how to use pressure points in negotiations.

active listening 10–11, 23–4
agreement 11–12
anger 13, 24, 60, 61–2, 64
auditory language 22, 23

back-up plans 50
balance of power 40–2, 43
bargaining 7–8
behaviour, difficult 46–7
bluffing 27, 29
body language 9, 16–32
  active listening 10, 23–4
  common mistakes 29–30
  congruence 27–8
  cultural differences 68–9
  facial expressions 16, 17, 20–1
  gestures 16, 17–19
  interpreting in context 26–7, 29, 30
  matching and mirroring 19–20
  phone negotiations 53
  props 25
  reaching agreement 12
  territory 28
breaks 11
business practices, cultural
  differences 72–4

clarifying position 12, 24, 57–8, 61,
  63
'closed' questions 6
co-operative negotiations 2–4, 35–6,
  39
communication see body language;
  language
competitive negotiations 2, 36, 38–9
concessions 2, 3
congruence, body language 27–8
context of negotiations 34–6, 43
correspondence 12, 59–60
cultural differences 17–18, 66–76

defence mechanisms 25
difficult negotiations 45
drinking etiquette, cultural differences
  70–1

e-mail negotiations 56–65
eating etiquette, cultural differences
  70–1
emotions, non-verbal communication
  24
empathy 10
eye contact 9, 10, 20–1, 24, 69
eyebrows, gestures 21

'face-savers' 37–8
facial expressions 16, 17, 20–1
fallback position 57
flexibility 58

gestures 16, 17–19
gifts, cultural differences 71
greeting people, cultural differences
  67–8
gustatory language 22, 23

hands, gestures 18
handshakes 12, 18–19
humour, cultural differences 71–2,
  75–6

industrial disputes 2
information-gathering 4–5, 13, 34, 43
interpreters 74

jokes, cultural differences 71–2, 75–6

kinaesthetic language 22, 23

language 9
  congruence 27–8

cultural differences 73–4
e-mail negotiations 62
vocabulary 21–3
leakage, body language 27–8, 29
letters 12, 59–60
listening 10–11, 23–4
lying 27–8, 29

matching and mirroring 19–20
meeting people, cultural differences
67–8

neurolinguistic programming (NLP)
21–2
non-verbal communication *see* body
language

objectives 4, 33, 42, 57
offers 8, 12
olfactory language 22, 23
'open-ended' questions 6
opening offers 5–6
bargaining 8
co-operative negotiations 3
competitive negotiations 2
e-mail negotiations 58

pay rises 77–86
performance reviews 77
personal space 28, 68
phone negotiations 50–3
planning negotiations 33–44
power, balance of 40–2, 43
'preening' 25

preparation 4–5, 34, 57
'problem-centred behaviour' 46–7
proposals 6–7
props, body language 25

questions:
'closed' 6
'open-ended' 6
power of 48–9

rapport, building 16–17, 20, 22
role-play, salary negotiations 79–80
rudeness, e-mail negotiations 61–2

salary negotiations 77–86
silence 11, 52, 68–9
social conventions, cultural
differences 67–72
'solution-centred behaviour' 46–7
summaries 12, 24, 58, 63

telephone negotiations 50–3
temper, losing 13, 24, 60, 61–2, 64
territory, body language 28
time, cultural differences 69
trading 6–7

visual language 22–3
visualisation, salary negotiations
79–80
vocabulary 21–3
vocal tone and pitch 16

women's roles, cultural differences 70